GIANT TORTOISE

By Janie Scheffer

Minneapolis, Minnesota

Credits

Cover and title page, © Dr Juergen Bochynek/iStock and © omkuhh/Adobe Stock; 3, © Gri-spb/iStock; 4–5, © Gerald and Buff Corsi Focus on Nature/iStock; 7, © GarySandyWales/iStock; 8T, © driftlessstudio/iStock; 8B, © Peyton Olesen/iStock; 11, © Fabian Ponce Garcia/Adobe Stock; 12–13, © Noelia Rivera/Adobe Stock; 14, © Tui De Roy/Minden Pictures; 15, © Tui De Roy/Minden Pictures; 17, © Chronicle/Alamy Stock Photo; 18–19, © chameleonseye/iStock; 21, © Soloviova Liudmyla/Adobe Stock; 23, © joreasonable/iStock

Bearport Publishing Company Product Development Team

Publisher: Jen Jenson; Director of Product Development: Spencer Brinker; Editorial Director: Allison Juda; Editor: Cole Nelson; Editor: Tiana Tran; Production Editor: Naomi Reich; Art Director: Kim Jones; Designer: Kayla Eggert; Designer: Steve Scheluchin; Production Specialist: Owen Hamlin

Statement on Usage of Generative Artificial Intelligence

Bearport Publishing remains committed to publishing high-quality nonfiction books. Therefore, we restrict the use of generative AI to ensure accuracy of all text and visual components pertaining to a book's subject. See BearportPublishing.com for details.

Library of Congress Cataloging-in-Publication Data

Names: Scheffer, Janie, 1992- author.
Title: Giant tortoise / by Janie Scheffer.
Description: Minneapolis, Minnesota : Bearport Publishing Company, [2025] | Series: Library of awesome animals | Includes bibliographical references and index.
Identifiers: LCCN 2025000161 (print) | LCCN 2025000162 (ebook) | ISBN 9798895770443 (library binding) | ISBN 9798895774687 (paperback) | ISBN 9798895771617 (ebook)
Subjects: LCSH: Testudinidae--Juvenile literature.
Classification: LCC QL666.C584 S34 2025 (print) | LCC QL666.C584 (ebook) | DDC 597.924--dc23/eng/20250207
LC record available at https://lccn.loc.gov/2025000161
LC ebook record available at https://lccn.loc.gov/2025000162

Copyright © 2026 Bearport Publishing Company. All rights reserved. No part of this publication may be reproduced in whole or in part, stored in any retrieval system, or transmitted in any form or by any means, electronic, mechanical, photocopying, recording, or otherwise, without written permission from the publisher. Bearport Publishing is a division of FlutterBee Education Group.

For more information, write to Bearport Publishing, 3500 American Blvd W, Suite 150, Bloomington, MN 55431.

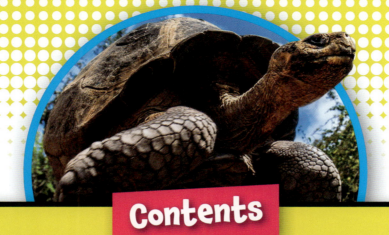

Contents

Awesome Giant Tortoises! 4
All in the Name 6
Two Shells 8
Cold-Blooded Creatures 10
Toothless Herbivores 12
Underground Nests 14
Hatchlings 16
Don't Eat Me! 18
Long Living 20

Information Station 22
Glossary 23
Index 24
Read More 24
Learn More Online 24
About the Author 24

AWESOME Giant Tortoises!

Ever so slowly, a huge, shelled animal moves across the ground. **STOMP!** Inch by inch, the giant tortoise makes its way, pushing along with short, sturdy legs. Slow and steady, giant tortoises are awesome!

IT WOULD TAKE A GIANT TORTOISE 25 MINUTES TO CROSS A FOOTBALL FIELD.

All in the Name

The giant tortoise's name says it all. This creature is massive! Of all tortoises, giant tortoises are the largest in the world. Fully grown, these creatures can weigh as much as a vending machine. They need strong, sturdy legs to support their heavy heads, shells, and tails.

> A GIANT TORTOISE'S LEGS ARE SO STRONG THAT THE BIG ANIMAL COULD EASILY CARRY AN ADULT HUMAN ON ITS BACK!

Two Shells

There are two **species** of giant tortoises, the Galápagos and the Aldabra. Both can live at sea level or high up in mountains, but the animals have different shells depending on the place they call home. Giant tortoises of either species that live in mountain **habitats** and eat small shrubs have dome-shaped shells. Those that live in lower areas and eat taller food, such as cacti, have **saddleback** shells.

> THOUGH THEY ARE BIG, GIANT TORTOISE SHELLS HAVE MANY SPACES THAT HOLD AIR. THIS MAKES THEM LIGHTER TO CARRY.

Cold-Blooded Creatures

Like all reptiles, giant tortoises are **cold-blooded**, meaning they cannot make their own body heat. To keep warm in cool weather, they lay out in the sun. During hot weather, giant tortoises sit in mud. *PLOP!* Mud helps block sunlight to keep the animals cool.

SITTING IN MUD ALSO HELPS PROTECT GIANT TORTOISES FROM MOSQUITOES.

Toothless Herbivores

What do giant tortoises eat? These huge reptiles are mostly **herbivores**. They eat plants, including cacti, fruits, and leaves. *MUNCH!* But this food doesn't give them much energy. So, the animals do everything very slowly. Giant tortoises even chew slowly, using the bony edges of their mouths to mash up food.

GIANT TORTOISES CAN GO WITHOUT FOOD OR WATER FOR UP TO A YEAR!

Underground Nests

Giant tortoises spend most of their lives alone. But once a year, the reptiles find one another to **mate**. This happens sometime between January and August. After mating, a tortoise mother finds a dry, sandy area to dig a nest. There, she lays her eggs.

GIANT TORTOISE EGGS ARE AS BIG AS TENNIS BALLS.

Hatchlings

A mother tortoise lays up to 25 eggs at a time. Then, she covers them with sand for protection. After more than 100 days, the eggs **hatch**. **CRACK!** Giant tortoise eggs at the bottom of the nest are warmer. When these hatchlings break out of their shells, they are female. The colder eggs on top become male hatchlings.

> TORTOISE HATCHLINGS USE A BUMP ON THEIR NOSE CALLED A CARUNCLE (KAHR-*uhng*-kuhl) TO BREAK OUT OF THEIR EGGSHELLS.

Don't Eat Me!

A tortoise's life isn't easy. From the very start, some eggs are eaten by **predators**, including rats, dogs, pigs, and cats. Those tortoises that do hatch may spend up to a month digging out of their sandy nests. For a long time, adult tortoises were also at risk from hunting. Humans killed some species until they were **extinct**. Many kinds of giant tortoises are still **endangered**.

TODAY, IT IS AGAINST THE LAW TO HUNT AND EAT GIANT TORTOISES.

Long Living

For those that make it to adulthood, giant tortoises have a long life ahead. These creatures are some of the longest-living land animals in the world. They often live for more than 100 years with some giant tortoises making it to almost 200 years old! That's some life!

THE WORLD'S OLDEST KNOWN GIANT TORTOISE, JONATHAN, IS MORE THAN 190 YEARS OLD!

21

Information Station

GIANT TORTOISES ARE AWESOME!
LET'S LEARN EVEN MORE ABOUT THEM.

Kind of animal: Giant tortoises are reptiles. They are cold-blooded animals with scaly skin that lay eggs.

More tortoises: There are 49 species of tortoises around the world. The speckled padloper is the smallest, growing to be only 3 inches (7.6 cm) long.

Size: Giant tortoises can grow up to 6 feet (1.8 m) long. That's about the length of a small sofa.

GIANT TORTOISES AROUND THE WORLD

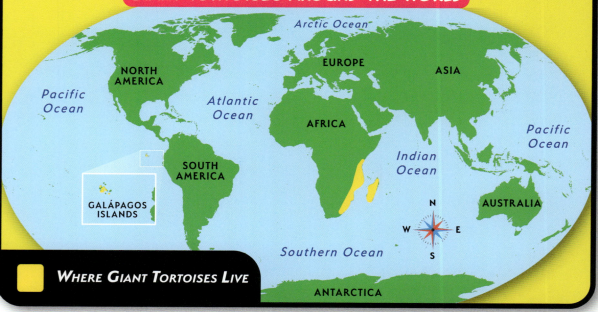

Where Giant Tortoises Live

22

Glossary

cold-blooded having a body temperature that changes with the temperature of the environment

endangered in danger of dying out completely

extinct no longer existing

female a giant tortoise that can lay eggs

habitats places in nature where animals normally live

hatch when a baby animal breaks out of its egg

herbivores animals that eat only plants

male a giant tortoise that cannot lay eggs

mate to come together to have young

predators animals that hunt other animals for food

species groups that animals are divided into, according to similar characteristics

Index

cold-blooded 10, 22	**female** 16	**male** 16
eggs 14, 16, 18, 22	**habitat** 8	**mate** 14
endangered 18	**hatchlings** 16, 18	**predators** 18
extinct 18	**herbivores** 12	**species** 8, 18, 22

Read More

Gendall, Megan. *Giant Tortoises (Reptiles).* Mendota Heights, MN: North Star Editions, 2024.

Pattison, Darcy. *Diego, the Galápagos Giant Tortoise: Saving a Species from Extinction (Another Extraordinary Animal).* Little Rock, AR: Mims House, 2022.

Learn More Online

1. Go to **FactSurfer.com** or scan the QR code below.
2. Enter "**Giant Tortoise**" into the search box.
3. Click on the cover of this book to see a list of websites.

About the Author

Janie writes books for kids and lesson plans for teachers. She loves nature hikes and taking her three kids to the zoo!